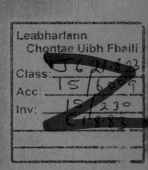

SIMPLE MACHINE PROJECTS

Making Machines with

Wheels and Axles

Chris Oxlade

raintree

a Capstone company — publishers for children

Raintree is an imprint of Capstone Global Library Limited, a company incorporated in England and Wales having its registered office at 7 Pilgrim Street, London, EC4V 6LB – Registered company number: 6695582

www.raintree.co.uk
myorders@raintree.co.uk

Edited by James Benefield and Erika Shores
Designed by Steve Mead
Original illustrations © Capstone Global Library Ltd 2015
Picture research by Jo Miller
Production by Victoria Fitzgerald
Originated by Capstone Global Library Ltd
Printed and bound in China

ISBN 978 1 406 28931 2
18 17 16 15 14
10 9 8 7 6 5 4 3 2 1

British Library Cataloguing in Publication Data
A full catalogue record for this book is available from the British Library.

Acknowledgements
We would like to thank the following for permission to reproduce photographs:

All photos Capstone Studio: Karon Dubke except: Dreamstime: Benjamin Gelman, 15; Getty Images: Tim Graham, 9; Shutterstock: fimkaJane, 29 (top), Jo De Vulder, 20, mertcan, 6, Monkey Business Images, 7, Pecold, 29 (bottom), Raimundas, 27, sydeen, 26, Tatiana Belova, 14, underworld, 4; UIG via Getty Images: Universal History Archive, 8.

Design Elements: Shutterstock: Timo Kohlbacher.

We would like to thank Harold Pratt and Richard Taylor for their invaluable help in the preparation of this book.

Every effort has been made to contact copyright holders of material reproduced in this book. Any omissions will be rectified in subsequent printings if notice is given to the publisher.

All the internet addresses (URLs) given in this book were valid at the time of going to press. However, due to the dynamic nature of the internet, some addresses may have changed, or sites may have changed or ceased to exist since publication. While the author and publisher regret any inconvenience this may cause readers, no responsibility for any such changes can be accepted by either the author or the publisher.

CONTENTS

Some words are shown in bold, **like this**. You can find out what they mean by looking in the glossary.

WHAT ARE WHEELS AND AXLES?

When you ride your bike, steer a go-kart or turn a tap on or off, wheels and **axles** are helping you. A wheel and axle is a simple machine. In this book, you'll see many examples of wheels and axles, from the everyday to the extraordinary. The projects will help you to understand how wheels and axles work.

The wheels and axles on a skateboard let the board roll easily along.

SIMPLE MACHINES

Simple machines make our lives easier by helping us to move and lift heavy loads, fix things tightly in place and cut tough materials. Wheels and axles are one of the five types of simple machines. The other four are the **pulley**, the **lever**, the **ramp** or the **wedge**, and the **screw**.

Wheels and axles around us

There are probably more wheels and axles around you than you think. Even a simple doorknob that you turn to open a door works with a wheel and axle. The diagram below explains a little more about these simple machines.

A wheel and axle is made up of a wheel joined to an axle (a rod).

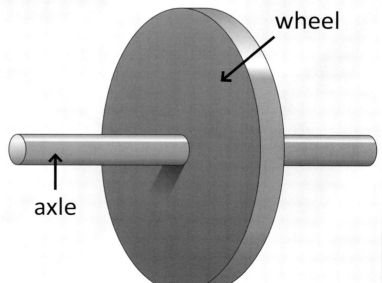

wheel

axle

HOW WHEELS AND AXLES WORK

Wheels and axles help us in two different ways. Here we look at how they help us to move things along. They also make forces larger (see the panel opposite), and change **motion** (see page 14).

Imagine pushing a heavy box along the ground, and then imagine pushing the box along on a skateboard. It's much easier to push it along on a skateboard. That's because wheels reduce **friction**. Friction is a force. It tries to stop surfaces sliding past one other. Friction makes it hard to push a heavy box along the ground. Rolling wheels make much less friction, so a box on wheels is easier to move.

A parcel trolley has wheels and axles that make it easy to move heavy boxes from one place to another.

FORCE AND MOTION

Simple machines such as wheels and axles can change force and motion. A simple machine can make a force (a push or a pull) larger or smaller, or change its direction. It can also make a movement (motion) larger or smaller, or change its direction.

 The wheels make it easy for these children to roll along.

WHEELS AND AXLES IN HISTORY

For many thousands of years, people moved objects by carrying them, by dragging them or by getting an animal to carry them. Things got a lot easier when the wheel was invented. We don't know who invented the wheel, or exactly when or where – but it was probably around 5,500 years ago in the Middle East. The first wheels were used on simple carts.

This picture carved over 2,500 years ago shows spoked wheels on a hunting chariot.

Wheels for pottery

As people started putting wheels on carts, potters realized they could make pots with a wheel. To do this, potters place a wheel on its side. They put a blob of clay on the wheel, and then turn the wheel. As the wheel turns, the potter presses on the clay to shape it into a neat circular pot.

WATER WHEELS

A water wheel is a large wheel with buckets around the rim. When water is poured into the buckets, the wheel turns. In the past, water wheels worked the **grindstones** in mills.

Potters have made pots on simple wheels like this for thousands of years.

Moving on wheels

In this project, you'll be able to see what the effect of adding wheels to something is.

What you need:
- a small cardboard box (about 20 cm long and about 10 cm across)
- some cotton thread
- a small plastic cup
- some marbles
- two long, sharp pencils
- some thick card
- sticky tape
- scissors

1 Cut a piece of cotton thread 10 cm long. Attach one end of the thread to the end of the box. Put the box on your worktop, a few centimetres back from the edge (see picture below).

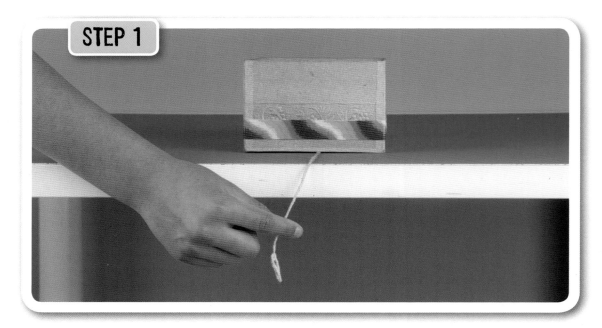

STEP 1

2 Hang the thread over the edge of the worktop. Tape the thread into the inside of the cup.

3 Put marbles into the cup one by one, until the box slides across the table (see picture below). Write down how many marbles you needed.

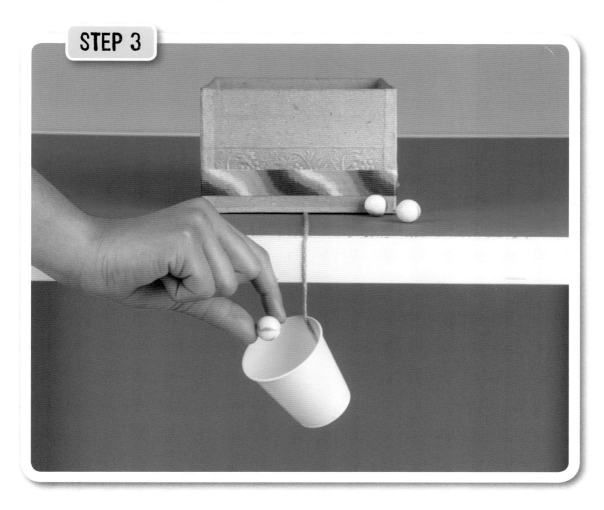

STEP 3

4 Using a sharp pencil, make two holes in each side of the box. Make the holes 2 cm up from the bottom of the box and 2 cm in from the ends of the box.

5 Wiggle the pencil around in the holes so that the pencils can spin easily (see picture, right).

STEP 5

6 Draw four circles about 8 cm across on thick card (you can use a tin can to draw around, if it's easier).

7 Cut out the circles carefully. Pierce a hole in the centre of each circle.

STEP 7

8 Put a pencil through the holes you pierced at each end of the box. Push the wheels onto the ends of the pencils.

9 The vehicle is complete. Place it 5 cm from the edge of the worktop, and hang the cotton thread and cup over the edge.

10 Put marbles into the cup again one by one until the box moves.

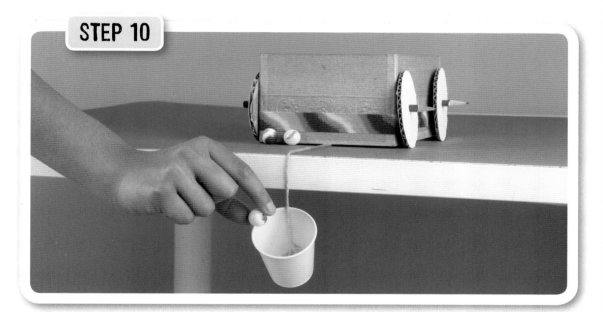

STEP 10

What did you find out?

Friction stopped the box from moving easily before you added the wheels. It took fewer marbles to make the box move after you added the wheels. This shows that the wheels reduced friction.

CHANGING FORCE AND MOTION

A wheel and axle can change the degree of force. This is because the **diameter** of the wheel is greater than the diameter of the axle. Think about the steering wheel on a go-kart. The steering wheel is on the end of a rod, which is its axle. Small up-and-down pushes and pulls on the steering wheel make much larger pushes and pulls on the axle. This makes it easy to steer the go-kart.

Can you find where the wheels and axles is on this go-kart?

Axles for spinning

Simple machines can also change motion. A simple spinning top (in the photo, below) is a wheel and axle. The triangle-like bottom part is the wheel and the top part, the spindle, is the axle. A small movement of your fingers makes it move quickly. This is because the wheel and axle increases the speed of movement.

spindle

This spinning top is made up of a wheel at the bottom and an axle at the top.

BALANCING WHEELS

A gyroscope (say "jie-ruh-scope") is a balancing device with a heavy wheel that spins to keep it steady. Pulling a string that's wrapped around the wheel's axle makes the wheel turn at very high speed.

Lifting with a wheel and axle

This simple project will help you to understand how a wheel and axle can make a force larger.

What you need:
- some thin card
- scissors
- sticky tape
- a long pencil
- cotton thread
- three identical washers

1 Cut a piece of card 25 cm long and 5 cm wide.

2 Tape one end of the card to the pencil, as shown in the picture (below).

STEP 2

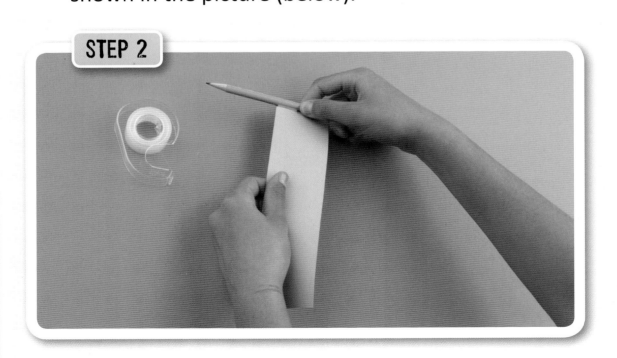

3 Wrap the card tightly around the pencil (see picture, below). Tape down the end of the card to stop the card from unwrapping.

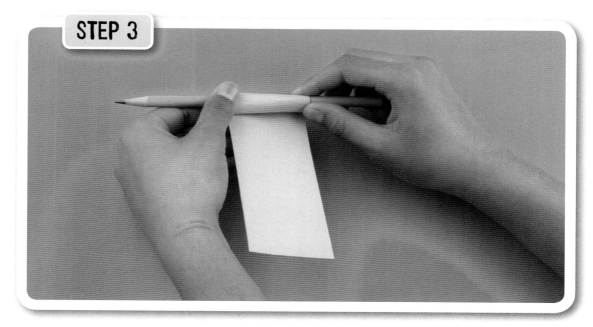

STEP 3

4 Cut another piece of card 25 cm long and 5 cm wide. Stick it on to the piece of wound up card and wrap it around as before. Cut and stick on a third piece of card in the same way. These pieces of rolled up card stuck around the pencil form a **drum**.

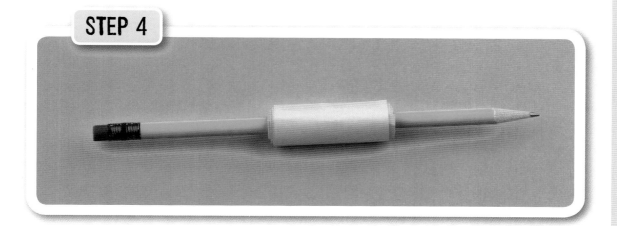

STEP 4

5 Cut two pieces of cotton thread, one about 1 metre long and one about 50 cm long.

6 Tape the end of the longer thread to the centre of the drum (see picture below).

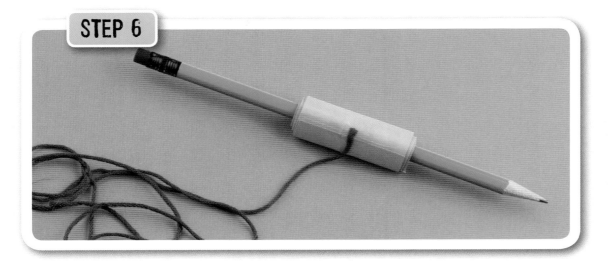

STEP 6

7 Tape a washer to the end of this cotton thread. Spin the pencil slowly to wind the thread onto the drum.

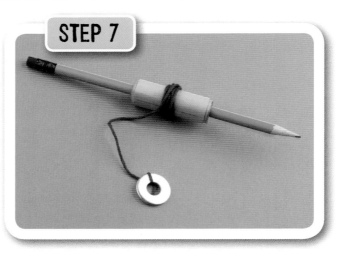

STEP 7

8 Now take the short thread and tape it to the pointed end of the pencil, as in the picture for step 9.

9 Tape two washers to the end of the shorter thread. Spin the pencil slowly to wind the thread. Spin it in the opposite direction to how you did it in step 7.

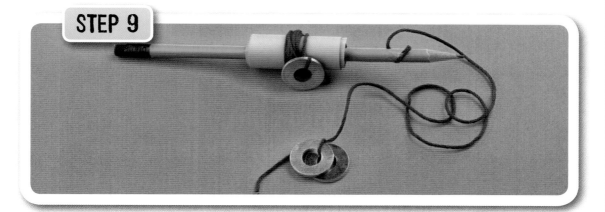

STEP 9

10 Hold the ends of the pencil like the picture and hold it at chest height. Release your grip to allow the pencil to spin.

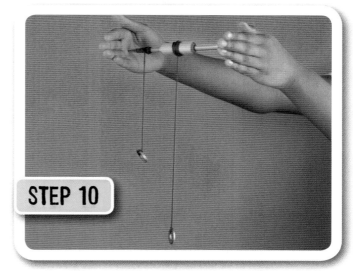

STEP 10

What did you find out?

The drum and pencil worked like a wheel and axle. The smaller weight on the thread around the drum (the wheel) lifted the larger weight on the thread around the pencil (the axle).

GEAR WHEELS

A **gear wheel** is a wheel with teeth around the rim (see the picture below).

Gear wheels are always used with other gear wheels. When the teeth of two gear wheels interlock, the wheels can turn one another. We use gear wheels to transfer movement from one axle to another. So when you turn one axle, the other axle turns, too.

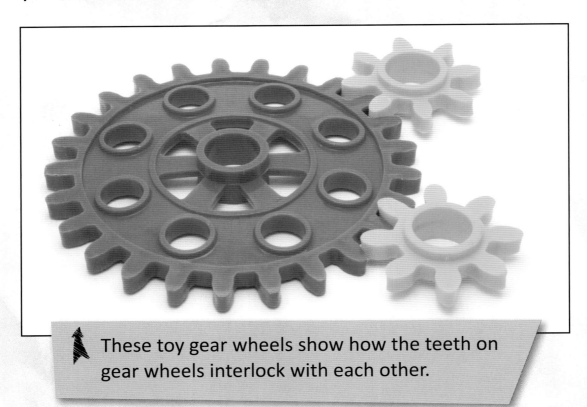

These toy gear wheels show how the teeth on gear wheels interlock with each other.

Changing speeds

We often use different sizes of gear wheels together. When you turn one wheel, the other wheel turns faster or slower than the first wheel. If the second wheel is larger, it turns more slowly. If the second wheel is smaller, it turns more quickly.

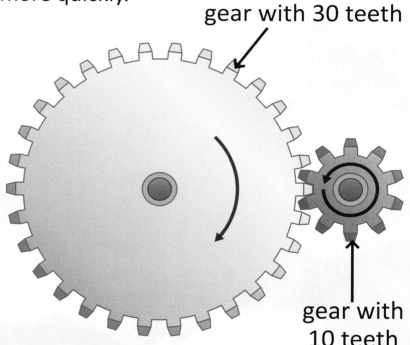

gear with 30 teeth

With these gear wheels, one turn of the large wheel turns the small wheel three times.

gear with 10 teeth

NANO GEARS

The word *nano* means "extremely small". Engineers have built experimental nano gear wheels that are too small to see with your eyes! They might be used in the future in tiny machines.

Making gear wheels

In this project, you will make two model gear wheels and see how they turn one another.

What you need:
- a CD or DVD (make sure it's an old one that you are allowed to use)
- a tin can
- two sharp pencils
- strong scissors
- some thick card
- 10 lolly sticks
- all-purpose glue

1 Draw around a CD on thick card. Cut out the circle.

2 Draw around a tin can that's about 8 cm across. Cut out the circle (see below for what the circles will look like).

STEP 2

3 On the large circle, draw lines at the positions of the 12 numbers on a clock face (ask an adult to help).

4 On the small circle, draw eight lines, equally spaced around the circle (see picture, right).

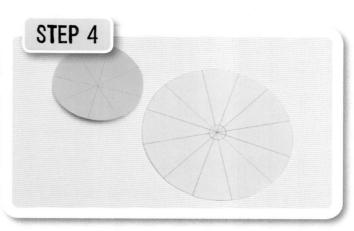

STEP 4

5 Draw a line 3 cm from the end of each lolly stick. Ask an adult to cut across the sticks at the lines with strong scissors (see picture below).

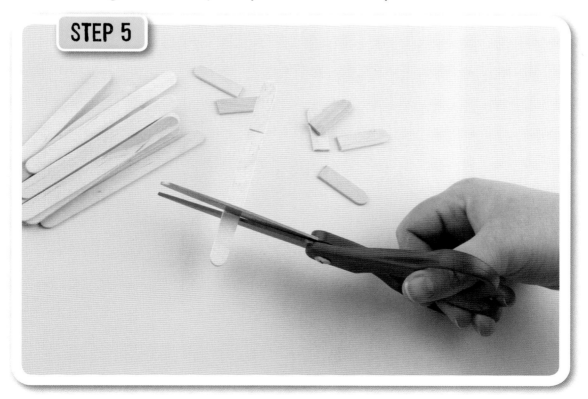

STEP 5

6 Glue a lolly stick end to one of the circles at the end of one of the lines, as shown in the picture below.

7 Now glue a lolly stick end on all the other lines. Turn the circles over and let the glue dry.

STEP 6

8 Cut a piece of card about 25 cm x 15 cm. Mark the halfway point up each of the shorter sides of the card, and draw a line to join these. Along this centre line, make two marks on the card, 11.5 cm across.

STEP 9

9 With a sharp pencil, pierce holes in the card at the two marks. Wiggle the pencil around until it can spin freely.

10 Push a pencil through the circles' centres.

11 Put the pencils through the holes in the sheet of card so that the gear wheels line up.

12 Turn the small wheel. The large wheel will turn, too.

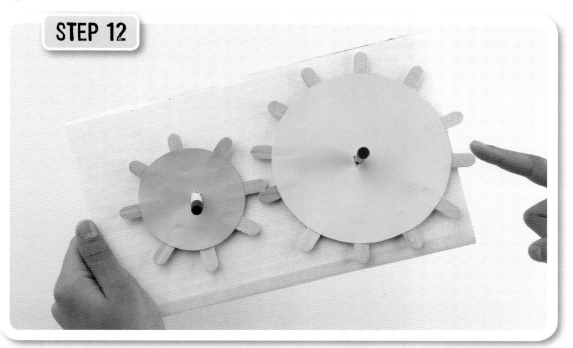

STEP 12

What did you find out?

You will see that the gear wheels turn in opposite directions. The wheels have a different number of teeth. It takes three turns of the small wheel to make the large wheel turn twice.

WHEELS AND AXLES IN COMPLEX MACHINES

Many complex machines are made up of simple machines such as wheels and axles.

Of course, complex machines such as lorries and trains need wheels and axles to move along roads or railway tracks. But they also have wheels and axles inside them. Engines and gearboxes are full of wheels, axles and gear wheels. These make forces larger and smaller, or make moving parts go faster or slower.

Gearboxes contain wheels and axles of different sizes.

Shaped wheels

Some machines contain wheels that are shaped to produce movement. These special wheels are called cams. As a cam turns, it pushes a lever up or lets it fall. You can see cams at work in some wooden toys.

CLOCK AND WATCH GEARS

Clocks and watches contain gears that control the speeds of the hands. A motor turns the second hand. Gears slow this movement down to move the minute hand and hour hand at the correct speeds.

 The inside of a clock contains wheels shaped to produce movement.

FACTS AND FUN

AMAZING WHEELS AND AXLES

The wheels on the world's largest dump truck (the 496 tonne Belaz 75710) are a monster 4 metres (13 feet) tall. The truck has eight wheels in total.

The world's largest working water wheel is the Laxey Wheel on the Isle of Man. It's an amazing 22.1 metres (72 feet) across – that's the same as the height of a seven-storey building.

In 2015, engineers will complete the world's largest ferris wheel (big wheel), the Dubai Wheel. It will be 210 metres (689 feet) across.

Scientists in Singapore have built a tiny, tiny gear wheel just 1.2 nanometres across. If 1 million of these gear wheels were lined up side by side, the line would be just over a millimetre long.

WHEELS AND AXLES TODAY

All simple machines, including wheels, were invented thousands of years ago. Wheels and axles are even more important today than they were in the past – we travel so much today. And wheels and axles will certainly be useful for many years to come!

What and where are the wheels and axles?

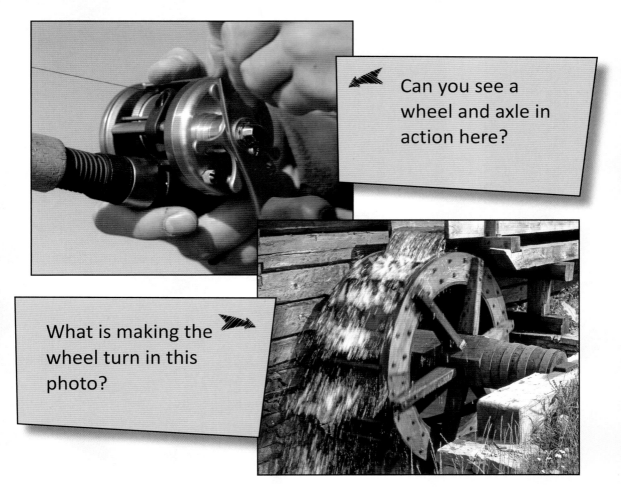

Can you see a wheel and axle in action here?

What is making the wheel turn in this photo?

GLOSSARY

axle rod that is attached to the centre of a wheel

diameter distance from one side of a circle to the other, which is measured from the centre

drum cylinder that a rope or string is wound around

friction force that tries to stop two touching surfaces (such as the floor and the sole of a shoe) from sliding past each other

gear wheel wheel that has teeth around its rim that interlock with the teeth on another gear wheel

grindstones two stones, one on top of the other, that grind wheat between them when the top wheel turns

lever long bar that is pushed or pulled against a fulcrum to help move heavy loads or cut material

motion movement

pulley simple machine made up of wheels and rope, used to lift or pull objects

ramp simple machine used to lift heavy objects

screw simple machine that has a spiral-shaped thread, used to fix or lift materials

wedge simple machine used to split apart materials

FIND OUT MORE

Books

Put Wheels & Axles to the Test, Sally M. Walker & Roseanne Feldmann (Lerner Classroom, 2011)

How Machines Work: The Interactive Guide to Simple Machines and Mechanisms, Nick Arnold (Running Press, 2011)

How Things Work (Simple Mechanisms), Ade Deane-Pratt (Wayland, 2011)

Websites

www.edheads.org/activities/simple-machines/index.shtml
Discover more about machines on this website.

www.galaxy.net/~k12/machines
There are plenty of simple machine projects to try on this site.

www.msichicago.org/fileadmin/Activities/Games/simple_ machines
This fun cartoon game is based on simple machine puzzles.

Video

mocomi.com/wheel-and-axle
Learn more about wheels and axles in this animation.

INDEX